Wetlands

Written by Lee Wang

Series Consultant: Linda Hoyt

WorldWise
Content-based Learning

Contents

Chapter 1

What is a wetland? 4

How do wetlands
fill up with water? 6

Saltwater wetlands 7

Freshwater wetlands 7

Chapter 2

**Surviving in a
watery world 8**

How wetland plants
survive 10

How wetland
animals survive 12

Chapter 3

The Okavango Delta 14

Seasonal changes
in the delta 15

People in the
Okavango Delta 16

The Nile crocodile
project 18

Chapter 4

Kakadu National Park 20

The flow of water in the Kakadu wetlands 22

A fragile ecosystem 23

Human activity in Kakadu 24

Conservation action helps protect the park 25

Chapter 5

Wetlands at risk 26

Why we should save wetlands 28

What you can do 30

Glossary 31

Index 32

Chapter 1

What is a wetland?

Wetlands are areas of land that are wet and watery. Some wetlands are always covered with water, while others dry out for part of the year. Wetlands are like giant sponges. They soak up excess water after heavy rains and help stop flooding. They also clean water by filtering out pollutants such as sewage and waste from farms, towns and factories. And they provide many animals and plants with a place to live and a supply of food.

In the past, many people thought that wetlands were no more than breeding areas for mosquitoes and that they should be drained. Over time, many wetlands were drained and filled in so that people could build houses, roads and towns.

 Did you know?

Wetlands provide **habitats** for about one-fifth of the world's known **species**.

4

▼ Crocodiles basking in the sun in the Pantanal wetlands in South America

The loss of wetlands has caused many problems. Many animals and plants that need them for their survival have become **endangered** because they have lost the places where they find food and shelter. Some of these plants and animals might die out altogether. When wetlands are destroyed, storm water and runoff after heavy rains have nowhere to drain into and can cause flooding in those areas.

Did you know?
The world's largest wetland is the Pantanal, which covers land in Brazil, Bolivia and Paraguay.

How do wetlands fill up with water?

A wetland is the area between dry land and a body of water such as a river, lake or the ocean. It is the area where water floods the land and the soil remains waterlogged. After heavy rainfall, rainwater flows over the land and into streams, rivers, lakes and **estuaries**. Some of this rainwater also soaks into the ground.

There are both saltwater and freshwater wetlands. Saltwater wetlands are found near the sea. Freshwater wetlands are found inland.

The amount of water in a wetland depends on these factors:

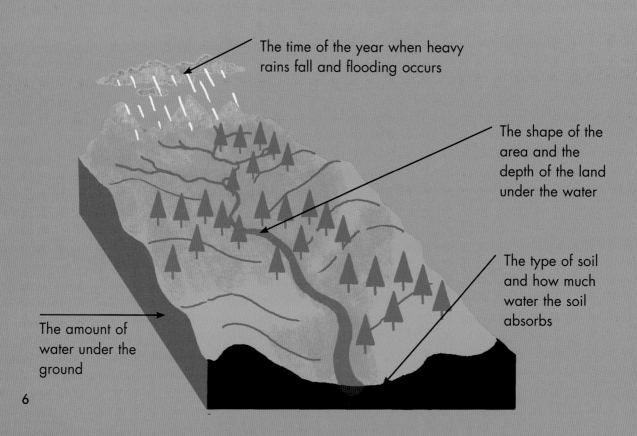

The time of the year when heavy rains fall and flooding occurs

The shape of the area and the depth of the land under the water

The type of soil and how much water the soil absorbs

The amount of water under the ground

Saltwater wetlands

Saltwater marshes

These wetlands are found where a river meets the sea in places with cooler climates. Mainly small plants such as grasses grow in salt marshes.

Mangrove swamps

Mangrove swamps are shallow saltwater wetlands found in coastal areas in warm tropical places.

Freshwater wetlands

Swamps

A swamp is a shallow wetland that often floods. It often has woody plants such as trees.

Freshwater marshes

A marsh is a wetland with shallow water. It usually has small plants such as grasses, reeds and water lilies.

Bogs

Bogs are found in cold places that are rainy. They often have poor drainage and the ground is wet and spongy.

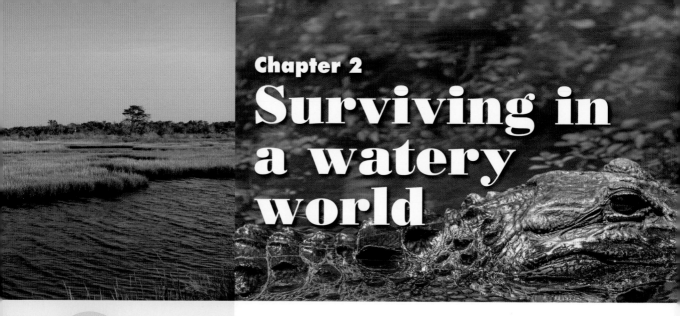

Chapter 2
Surviving in a watery world

Did you know?

Water lilies have large flowers that have seeds. When the lilies have finished flowering, these seeds float away to other parts of the wetland and grow into new plants.

Wetlands provide a place where plants and animals live together. Because many wetlands expand in the wet season and shrink in the dry season, the plants and animals that live there have adapted to survive these seasonal changes.

The kinds of plants that are found in wetlands depend on the amount of water, how deep it is, and the features these plants have developed that allow them to survive in wet places.

Wetland plants produce food such as seeds that animals eat. As well as providing food, the plants in wetlands provide shelter and places for animals to breed. Fish, mammals and **migrating** birds find food and shelter in wetlands. Fish and amphibians lay their **spawn** in wetlands.

A wetlands environment

Many animals are found at the edge.

conifers

cottonwoods

grasses

rushes

sedges

mud flats

water lilies

bulrushes

sedges

rushes

Many plants are found at the edge.

The water is deeper in the middle than it is at the edge.

The bottom of a wetland is mud. This mud is made from soil, and dead plants and animals. There is lots of food for animals and plants in this mud.

How wetland plants survive

Most green plants need these things to grow: light, air, water, warmth from the sun, and food or **nutrients**. Most plants that grow on land take in air through their roots from the spaces in the soil.

Wetland plants grow in water or in very wet soil where there is little or no air. To survive, these plants take in air through their leaves and down their hollow, spongy stems to their roots.

Surviving seasonal changes

Plants such as grasses, sedges and rushes grow in extremely wet soil. Their roots and stems are usually underwater in the mud and their leaves are in the air. These plants are called emergents. The stems of these plants can grow sideways through the mud.

Each year, the stems grow fresh shoots above the water to collect the sun's energy and make food, which is then stored underground in the roots and stems. In the dry season, the shoots die but the stems survive.

▲ Water lilies have air sacs in their stems. These get air to their roots in the mud and also help the lilies float.

◀ Reeds take in air through their leaves and hollow, woody stems. This helps the air reach their underground roots.

Surviving in salt water

Mangroves are trees that grow in mudflats in salty water near the sea. These trees can stop or reduce the entry of salt into their systems. They also have large roots that grow down and small roots that grow upwards through the mud into the air.

Mangroves take in air through small gaps in the bark and through special breathing pores in roots that grow above the water.

Insect eaters

Some plants live in waterlogged soil that contains very few nutrients. Carnivorous or insect-eating plants overcome this problem by trapping insects and dissolving them in a liquid. They get the food they need from these insects.

▲ Mangroves grow in water.

▼ Venus flytraps have leaves that look like a trap. When an insect crawls on the leaves, tiny hairs tell the plant something is there. The leaves close quickly around the insect just like a trap.

▲ Pitcher plants have a long hollow tube with water in the bottom. Insects crawl into this tube, fall to the bottom, and drown in the water.

11

How wetland animals survive

Many animals use wetlands. Some animals live there all the time. Others visit during the dry season for food, water and to breed. Animals that use wetlands have special features that help them to live in wetlands.

Mammals

Hippopotamuses live in wetland pools all year round. During the day, they rest in water, while at night they leave the water to eat grass. Deer and marsh rabbits have feet that spread out to stop them from getting stuck in the mud.

Birds

Many wading birds that live in wetlands have long legs for wading in the water where they catch food. Spoonbills have long beaks with a rounded end like a spoon. As they walk in shallow water, they swing their heads from side to side, taking fish and tiny animals from the water with their beaks.

12

Amphibians

Amphibians such as frogs and newts begin life in the water and move out of the water when they become adults. Frogs spend the first part of their lives swimming in water as tadpoles. They eat small pond plants. As they grow, they change from tadpoles into frogs. They grow legs, their tails disappear, and they grow lungs. These lungs let them leave the water and breathe air. Frogs eat insects that live in wetlands.

Reptiles

Reptiles such as turtles have webbed feet to help them swim in the water. Turtles grab small animals, insects and plants with their horny bills.

Fish

When the dry season starts, many wetland fish swim to deeper pools that do not dry up.

◀ The lungfish covers itself in a protective cocoon and buries itself in the mud to stop from drying out when the pools dry up. These fish remain buried for months, breathing air. When it rains and the pool fills with water, they come out of the mud.

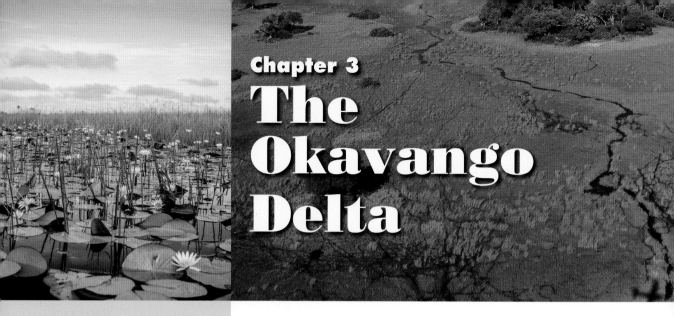

Chapter 3
The Okavango Delta

Fact file

Location: Botswana, Africa

Size of delta: 15,000 square kilometres

Climate: Summer (November to March) Winter (May to August)

Rainfall: Summer rainy season; winter dry

The Okavango Delta in Botswana, Africa is one of the largest inland wetlands of the world. This vast network of rivers, wet grassy land called marshes, and dry grasslands sits in the middle of the Kalahari Desert. The delta is fan shaped because the river spreads out in a fan-like pattern of dry land, marshes, and swamps. Some marshes are permanent, while others are seasonal and dry out during the dry season.

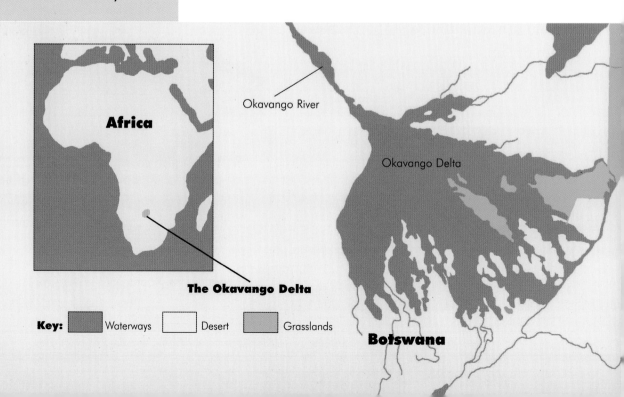

Africa

The Okavango Delta

Okavango River

Okavango Delta

Botswana

Key: Waterways   Desert   Grasslands

Seasonal changes in the delta

Some animals live year-round in the permanent marshes and swamps of this delta. These include hippopotamuses, crocodiles, antelopes and birds of prey.

Many animals travel to the delta each year in winter during the dry season to find water and fresh food to graze on. Millions of flamingos, spoonbills and waterfowl travel to the delta to find food.

Animals such as giraffes, zebras, elephants, buffaloes, kudu and wildebeests also leave the dry grasslands and travel to the delta for water in the waterholes. These birds and animals become food for **predators** such as lions, hyenas and crocodiles.

Plants and animals in the delta

Plants: 1,300 **species**
Mammals: 122 species
Reptiles: 64 species
Birds: 440 species
Amphibians: 33 species
Fish: 71 species

People in the Okavango Delta

The Okavango Delta also provides water, food and shelter for many people – over 140,000 people live in the delta. Many people live in small villages of fewer than 500 people. They rely on the delta's fresh water for growing food, drinking, food preparation, washing and transportation. They build their houses from reeds gathered from the wetlands.

Local farmers raise cattle in the Okavango Delta. The cattle industry is expanding to provide food for the growing **population**. Some people are concerned that the expansion of the cattle industry might threaten the delta's **ecosystem**. The cattle ranchers build fences to protect the cattle, but these fences stop the wild animals from reaching the waterholes in the delta during the dry season. Also when there are bushfires, wild animals can be trapped by the fences and cannot escape the fires.

? Did you know?

Unlike most rivers that flow from the mountains to the sea, a river flows inland and forms the Okavango Delta.

Crop farms around the Okavango Delta also pose a threat to the ecosystem. Crop farms use pesticides and fertilisers that can pollute the water. Crop farms also need water. Farmers often have to change the flow of water from one area to their farms to water their crops. This is called irrigation. If the water from the Okavango Delta is used to irrigate crop farms, parts of the Okavango Delta might dry out and this will damage the delta. Many conservationists are working to protect the health of the Okavango Delta.

Okavango wild dog project

The Okavango wild dog is an **endangered** species. Many dogs have been killed by local people because the dogs wander into villages and kill their livestock.

A project has been set up to protect these dogs. Project workers use radio technology to follow dog packs. They collect samples of the dogs' **scent markings** and stake out the boundaries of the pack's **territory**. The scent-mark samples are then placed outside villages to stop wild dog packs from entering the villages and killing livestock.

17

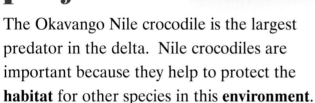

The Nile crocodile project

The Okavango Nile crocodile is the largest predator in the delta. Nile crocodiles are important because they help to protect the **habitat** for other species in this **environment**. These crocodiles eat the carnivorous fish that live in the delta. These fish eat other fish, which are also food for birds. Without the crocodiles, the carnivorous fish would overpopulate and eat all the other fish, and there would be no fish left for the birds. Crocodiles also eat dead animals, and this helps stop the dead animals from polluting the water in a lagoon or waterhole.

Scientists are helping teach people about the importance of the Nile crocodile. They have introduced programs for students in Botswana to share information about Nile crocodiles with students around the world.

Nile crocodile
Weight: Average 225 kilograms; some weigh up to 730 kilograms
Size: Average 5 metres; some grow to 6 metres
Lifespan: Approximately 45 years

Lucie Evans tells of her experience working on a volunteer research project to study crocodiles and the environment in which they live.

The two-week project, in the Okavango Delta in Botswana, consisted mainly of capturing crocodiles within the channels and lagoons of the Okavango River.

This task was undertaken at night, by boat, with a spotlight to sweep the banks and the river surface where crocodiles reveal their presence with glowing orange eyes. After fixing the crocodile's gaze with the light beam, they were captured by hand or noose according to their size, and then examined, measured and weighed.

The raised scales along the back and tail (scutes) were cut in a specific pattern to enable future identification (a painless exercise, just like cutting our fingernails), samples of blood and urine were taken, and the crocodile's position was recorded using a **GPS** (global positioning system) unit. The crocodiles were then released back into their habitat.

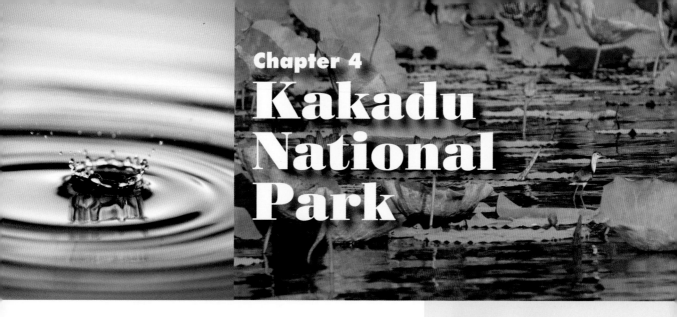

Chapter 4
Kakadu National Park

Kakadu National Park in the Northern Territory, Australia contains huge wetlands. Most of the water in Kakadu comes from heavy rains from November to March. This is the wet season that brings monsoonal rain. The water fills creeks and rivers, flows into the lagoons and swamps and floods the plains. At this time, waterfalls on the **escarpment** become roaring torrents. During the dry season, when very little rain falls, the wetland dries up quite a lot. The only water that remains is in lagoons and **billabongs**.

? Did you know?

The three Alligator Rivers in Kakadu were given their names by Phillip Parker King, an English navigator in the early 1800s. He saw a large number of crocodiles that he mistook for alligators.

Fact file

Location: 120 kilometres east of Darwin, Northern Territory

Area: 19,757 square kilometres

Rainy season: November to March

Average rainfall: 130 to 156 centimetres

1981: Listed as a World Heritage site

1987, 1992: Extended and relisted as a World Heritage site

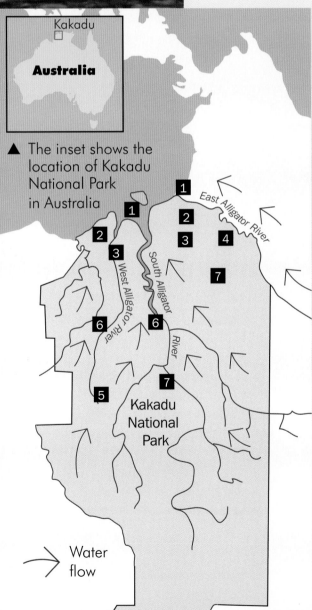

▲ The inset shows the location of Kakadu National Park in Australia

1 **Estuaries** are where the rivers run into the sea. The freshwater from the river mixes with the salty seawater. The sea floor is covered in sea grass, which shelters fish, turtles and shellfish, and also has coral and sea sponges.

2 Mangroves (39 different **species**) grow in the salt water of coastal rivers. During the dry season, many wading birds find food and shelter here.

3 Low shrubby vegetation grows on the tidal flats behind the mangroves.

4 Pockets of monsoonal forest grow along the river banks.

5 Eucalypts grow in open forests and **woodland** with tall (1- to 2-metre) grasses growing under them. When bushfires sweep through, only the outer bark burns and the trees survive. Huge termite mounds are found in the woodlands. Termites move to the top of these mounds when the floods come during the wet season.

6 Paperbark trees grow along rivers and swamps, and on low floodplains.

7 Swamps filter out pollution.

The flow of water in the Kakadu wetlands

The water levels in Kakadu are not the same all year round. Plants and animals have adapted to the alternating wet and dry seasons.

Season	Dry – winter	Wet – summer
When	**May to December**	**November to April**
Water level	Water levels start to drop and a series of lagoons and billabongs form.	Water levels rise after heavy monsoon rains. Most of Kakadu is covered with water and floating aquatic plants.
Animal life	Fish swim to deeper lagoons and billabongs during the dry season.

Towards the end of the dry season up to two million migratory waterbirds nest and breed in Kakadu. They eat the fish in the lagoons and billabongs.

Female freshwater crocodiles breed during the dry season. They lay their eggs in the sandy riverbanks.

The large predators such as crocodiles have an abundant supply of food. Birds, snakes and fish eat crocodile hatchlings. | Animals live throughout the park as there is plenty of water.

Insects, fish and saltwater crocodiles breed and this replenishes the food chain. Most fish breed around the beginning of the wet season.

Female saltwater crocodiles use tall dry reeds, leaves, mud and grasses to build their large nest mounds on a firm muddy bank. Some nests and eggs are destroyed by flooding. |

A fragile ecosystem

The Kakadu estuary is a fragile **ecosystem** that provides a nursery for many sea creatures. Marine life such as fish and prawns come to the estuary to breed.

The two most important types of plants in the estuary are mangroves and sea grasses. During the dry winter months, wading birds visit the mangroves to feed on sea creatures such as shrimp and fish, and many birds nest in the mangrove trees.

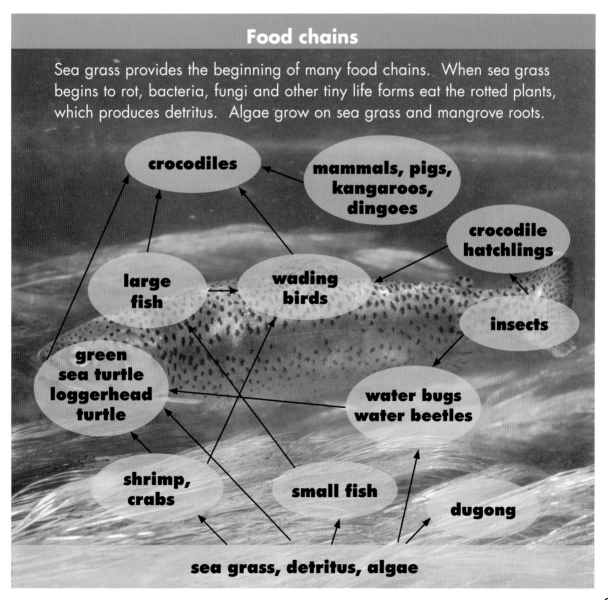

Food chains

Sea grass provides the beginning of many food chains. When sea grass begins to rot, bacteria, fungi and other tiny life forms eat the rotted plants, which produces detritus. Algae grow on sea grass and mangrove roots.

crocodiles

mammals, pigs, kangaroos, dingoes

crocodile hatchlings

large fish

wading birds

insects

green sea turtle loggerhead turtle

water bugs water beetles

shrimp, crabs

small fish

dugong

sea grass, detritus, algae

Human activity in Kakadu

Indigenous people have lived in the area now called Kakadu for more than 60,000 years. When Europeans settled here, they introduced animals from other countries that have damaged **habitats** and native animals. Water buffalo with hoofed feet trample and destroy the habitat of freshwater species. Thousands of feral pigs live on the edges of the floodplains and destroy the habitat.

Another threat to Kakadu has been the possibility of pollution from the Ranger uranium mine. There are strict environmental laws about how the mine operates and how mine water is released but pollution from the mine is still a possibility.

▲ Feral pigs feast in the wetland grasses.

Did you know?

Eleven wildlife species in Kakadu are endangered because of the loss of or damage to their habitats.

▼ Loggerhead turtle

Some species of turtles that nest along the coastlines of the park are endangered. They can be killed or harmed by swallowing sea debris or by getting entangled in fishing nets.

Conservation action helps protect the park

Conservation groups have been concerned about the damage to Kakadu National Park. They have lobbied the government to expand areas of the national park to protect habitats and wildlife. Kakadu has been listed as a World Heritage site because of its natural and cultural significance. The southern part of the park contains a number of art sites. This art provides information about Indigenous culture and the way the environment has changed over thousands of years. People can visit the national park all year round. They can learn more about this environment as they take part in activities like walking, canoeing and boat tours to view the wide range of plants and animals.

▲ Aboriginal rock art, Kakadu

▼ Saltwater crocodile　　　　▼ Freshwater crocodile

Today, saltwater and freshwater crocodiles are protected species in Australia because they have been hunted for many years. They are most common in tidal rivers, creeks and billabongs, so swimming for tourists is forbidden in parts of the park.

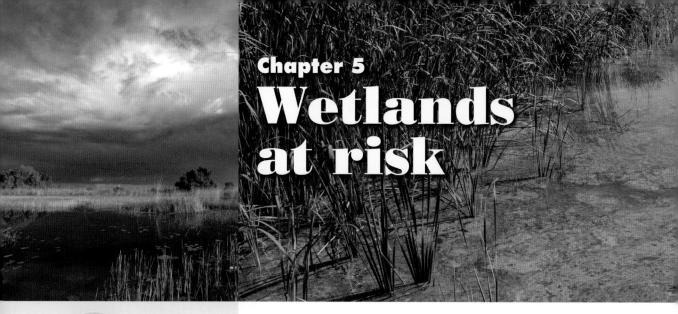

Chapter 5
Wetlands at risk

Did you know?

The world has lost half the wetlands that existed in the year 1900.

Over time people have damaged or destroyed many wetland areas. They have been used for farming, housing and roads. Wetlands have been drained, filled in and built on for urban development. **Canals** have been dug to divert water from wetland areas to urban areas. This kind of land use has had harmful effects on wetland **habitats** throughout the world.

▼ This satellite picture shows Hurricane Katrina over Louisiana in 2005.

▼ Flooding caused by Hurricane Katrina

Wetlands of international importance

In 1971, conservationists met in the city of Ramsar in Iran, where they made a list of wetlands that needed to be protected. This list is known as the Ramsar List of Wetlands of International Importance. Conservationists meet every three years to add wetlands to the list. There are now over 1,400 Ramsar sites.

Many coastal wetlands have been changed to allow for houses and roads to be built. The huge floods that swept into the city of New Orleans, Louisiana, USA, when Hurricane Katrina happened, are an example of how much damage can be caused when wetlands and marshes are removed or changed.

Human activities that can damage wetlands include:

- Building roads

- Clearing land

- Building suburbs and towns

- Polluting water

- Polluting air

- Using pesticides

- Irrigating land

- Building **levees** and canals

- Diverting water from creeks, rivers or streams.

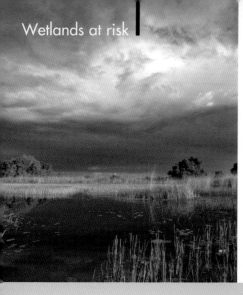

Why we should save wetlands

We must do whatever we can to save all wetland habitats because they are essential to the survival of many different types of wildlife. Wetlands provide many animals with food and water, as well as a place for them to breed, nest and raise their young – and a place to stop off when travelling or **migrating**.

Given that so many animals use the wetlands, it is crucial that people find out more about these fragile **ecosystems** and try to save them from being drained and used to build roads, farms and towns.

Birds

One-third of all bird **species** in North America depend on wetlands. Birds such as wild ducks and geese rest in wetlands during their annual migration. They also breed in wetlands. They care for their young in the wetlands, where they find food. In winter, many birds use wetland plants to nest, and to shelter from **predators**.

Mammals

Large numbers of mammals use wetlands to gather food and find protection.

Amphibians

Approximately 190 species of amphibians use wetlands to reproduce. Amphibians, such as frogs and salamanders, find a rich supply of food such as algae and small **invertebrates** in shallow ponds, where they are safe from predatory fish.

Freshwater fish

Many freshwater fish use the flood plains of larger rivers as places to **spawn** their eggs, and to raise and feed their young.

Marine animals

Many sea fish lay their spawn, and raise and feed their young in coastal wetlands. Shellfish, such as oysters, clams and shrimp, feed and protect their young in coastal wetlands.

What you can do

Many good things are now being done to save wetlands. People are now more aware of the importance of wetlands and are doing things to help save them.

Wetland conservation

Here are some ways that individuals can help save wetland areas:

- Volunteer to monitor and record wetland wildlife **populations**

- Protect the habitat in wetlands near where you live

- Join a local wetland **conservation** project

- Learn about wetlands – subscribe to a conservation magazine

- Stop using chemicals such as fertilisers and pesticides that kill plants or make animals sick.

Glossary

billabongs   waterholes in rivers that dry up when it is not the wet season

canals   waterways that have been built by people

conservation   to act to keep animals, plants or landforms in their natural state

detritus   plant or animal material that has decomposed

ecosystem   a whole community of living things that depend on each other for survival

endangered   a plant or animal that may soon become extinct

environment   all of the living things and non-living things that are together in a particular place

escarpment   a long cliff-like piece of rock

estuaries   marshes along coastlines where salty sea water mixes with fresh water from the inland

GPS   global positioning system; an electronic device that sends out and receives information about the location and movement of animals

habitats   places where a plant or an animal naturally lives

invertebrates   shrimp, lobsters, crabs, molluscs, worms; animals with no backbone

levees   artificial banks that have been built to stop flooding

migrating   moving from one place to another in a pattern each season

nutrients   different types of food that keep things alive

population   the number of people, plants or animals in a group, country or species

predators   animals that kill and eat other animals

scent markings   urine that animals leave to mark their territory

spawn   the eggs that animals such as frogs and toads lay in water

species   a group of closely related animals that can reproduce with each other

territory   an area of land that a group of animals claims as its own

woodland   an area of land covered with smaller trees and shrubs

Index

animals 4, 5, 8, 9, 12–13, 15, 16, 18, 22, 23, 24, 25, 28, 29, 30

conservation 17, 25, 27, 30, 31

dry season 8, 10, 12, 13, 14, 15, 16, 22

ecosystem 16, 17, 21, 23, 25, 28, 31

estuaries 6, 20, 22, 23, 25, 31

flooding 4, 5, 6, 26

food 4, 5, 8, 9, 10, 11, 12, 15, 16, 18, 22, 23, 28, 29

freshwater wetlands 6, 7

grasslands 14, 15, 20

habitats 4, 18, 19, 24, 25, 26, 28, 30, 31

Kakadu National Park 20–25

mangrove 7, 11, 21, 23, 25

marsh 7, 14, 15, 21, 22, 27

Nile crocodile 18–19

nutrients 10, 11, 31

Okavango Delta 14–19

Okavango wild dog 17

people 4, 16–17, 18, 24–25, 26, 28, 30

plants 4, 5, 7, 8, 9, 10–11, 13, 15, 22, 23, 24, 25, 28, 30

pollution 21, 24

predators 15, 18, 22, 28, 31

saltwater wetlands 6, 7

shelter 5, 8, 16, 20, 21, 23, 28

swamp 7, 14, 15

wet season 8, 20, 22

World Heritage site 21, 25